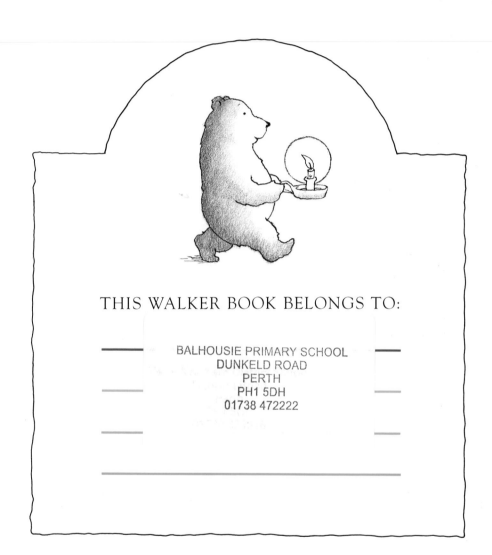

THIS WALKER BOOK BELONGS TO:

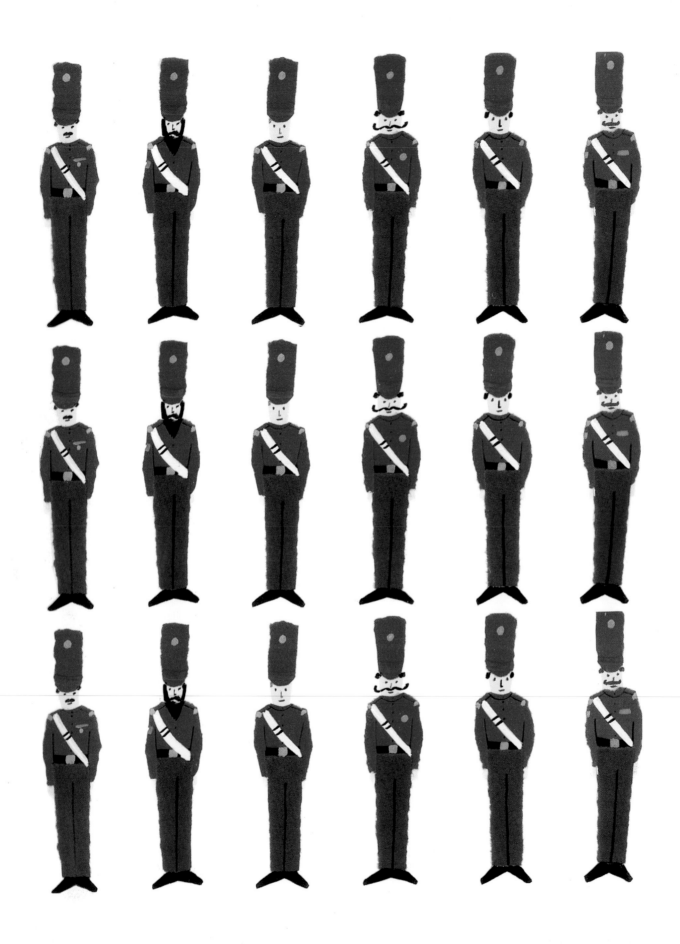

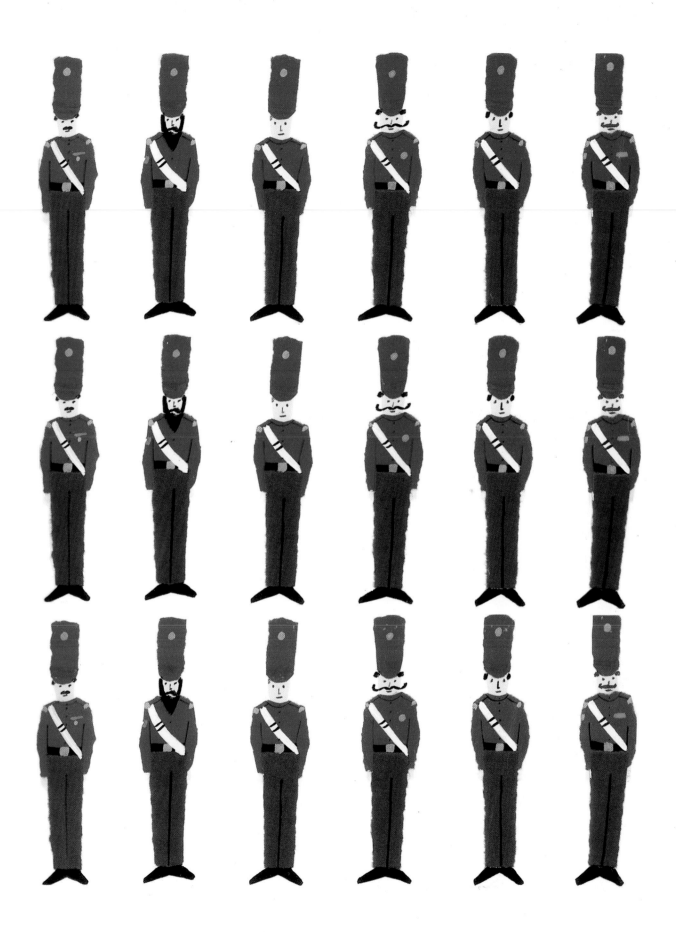

First published 1989 by Walker Books Ltd
87 Vauxhall Walk, London SE11 5HJ

This edition published 1997

2 4 6 8 10 9 7 5 3

© 1989 Julie Lacome

This book has been typeset in Times

Printed in Hong Kong

British Library Cataloguing in Publication Data
A catalogue record for this book is
available from the British Library.

ISBN 0-7445-5427-6

Sing a Song of Sixpence

and other nursery songs

Julie Lacome

WALKER BOOKS

AND SUBSIDIARIES

LONDON • BOSTON • SYDNEY

Sing a song of sixpence,
   A pocket full of rye,
Four and twenty blackbirds,
   Baked in a pie.

When the pie was opened,
   The birds began to sing;
Was not that a dainty dish
   To set before the king?

The king was in his counting-house,
   Counting out his money;
The queen was in the parlour,
   Eating bread and honey.

The maid was in the garden,
   Hanging out the clothes,
When down came a blackbird
   And pecked off her nose.

Here we go round the mulberry bush,
The mulberry bush, the mulberry bush,
Here we go round the mulberry bush,
On a cold and frosty morning.

This is the way we wash our hands,
Wash our hands, wash our hands,
This is the way we wash our hands,
On a cold and frosty morning.

This is the way we brush our teeth,
Brush our teeth, brush our teeth,
This is the way we brush our teeth,
On a cold and frosty morning.

This is the way we comb our hair,
Comb our hair, comb our hair,
This is the way we comb our hair,
On a cold and frosty morning.

Jack and Jill went up the hill,
    To fetch a pail of water;
Jack fell down and broke his crown,
    And Jill came tumbling after.

Then up Jack got and home did trot,
As fast as he could caper;
And went to bed to mend his head
With vinegar and brown paper.

Little Boy Blue,
Come blow your horn,
The sheep's in the meadow,
The cow's in the corn.

Where is the boy
   Who looks after the sheep?
He's under a haystack
   Fast asleep.
Will you wake him?
   No, not I,
For if I do,
   He's sure to cry.

Hickory, dickory, dock,
The mouse ran up the clock.
The clock struck one,
The mouse ran down;
Hickory, dickory, dock.

Hush, little baby, don't say a word,
Papa's going to buy you a mocking bird.

If the mocking bird won't sing,
Papa's going to buy you a diamond ring.

If the diamond ring turns to brass,
Papa's going to buy you a looking-glass.

If the looking-glass gets broke,
Papa's going to buy you a billy-goat.

If that billy-goat runs away,
Papa's going to buy you another today.

Row, row, row your boat,
   Gently down the stream;
Merrily, merrily, merrily, merrily,
   Life is but a dream.

See, saw, Margery Daw,
Johnny shall have a new master;
He shall have but a penny a day,
Because he can't work any faster.

Humpty Dumpty
  Sat on a wall,
Humpty Dumpty
  Had a great fall.

All the king's horses
  And all the king's men
Couldn't put Humpty
  Together again.

Yankee Doodle came to town,
　Riding on a pony;
He stuck a feather in his cap
　And called it macaroni.

Yankee Doodle keep it up,
　Yankee Doodle dandy;
Mind the music and the step,
　And with the girls be handy.

Baa baa black sheep, have you any wool?
  Yes sir, yes sir, three bags full:
One for the master and one for the dame,
  And one for the little boy who lives down the lane.

Hey diddle, diddle, the cat and the fiddle,
The cow jumped over the moon.
   The little dog laughed to see such sport,
And the dish ran away with the spoon.

Little Bo-Peep has lost her sheep,
And doesn't know where to find them;
Leave them alone and they'll come home,
Bringing their tails behind them.

Little Bo-Peep fell fast asleep,
And dreamt she heard them bleating;
But when she awoke, she found it a joke,
For they were still a-fleeting.

Then up she took her little crook,
  Determined for to find them;
She found them indeed, but it made her heart bleed,
  For they'd left all their tails behind them.

    It happened one day as Bo-Peep did stray
      Into a meadow hard by;
    There she espied their tails side by side,
      All hung on a tree to dry.

        She heaved a sigh and wiped her eye,
          Then went o'er hill and dale,
        And tried what she could, as a shepherdess should,
          To tack to each sheep its tail.

Hush-a-bye baby, on the tree top,
When the wind blows the cradle will rock;
When the bough breaks the cradle will fall,
Down will come baby, cradle, and all.

Twinkle, twinkle, little star,
How I wonder what you are!
Up above the world so high,
Like a diamond in the sky.
Twinkle, twinkle, little star,
How I wonder what you are!

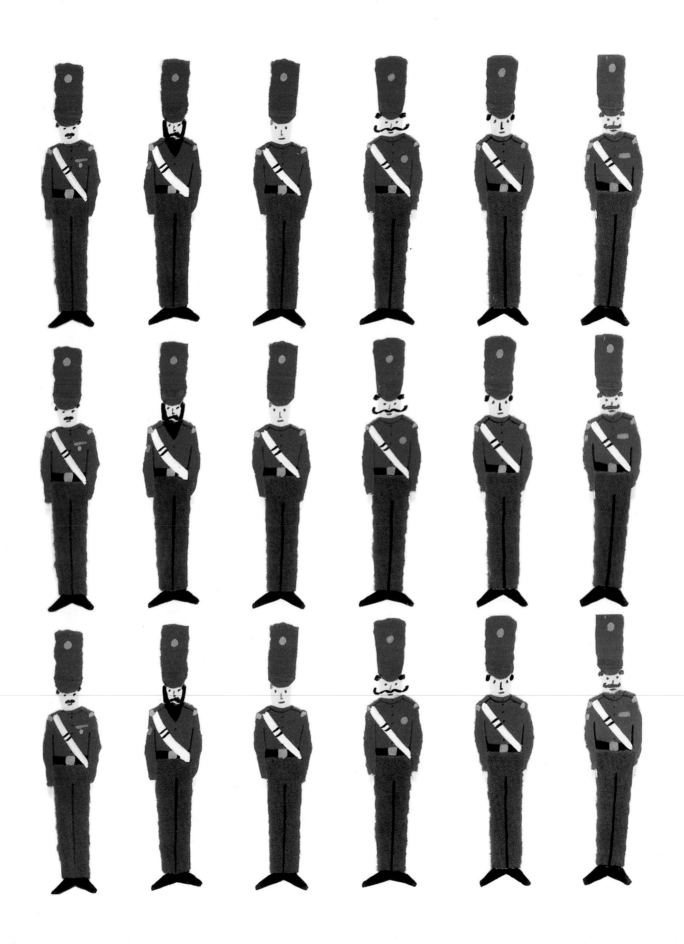

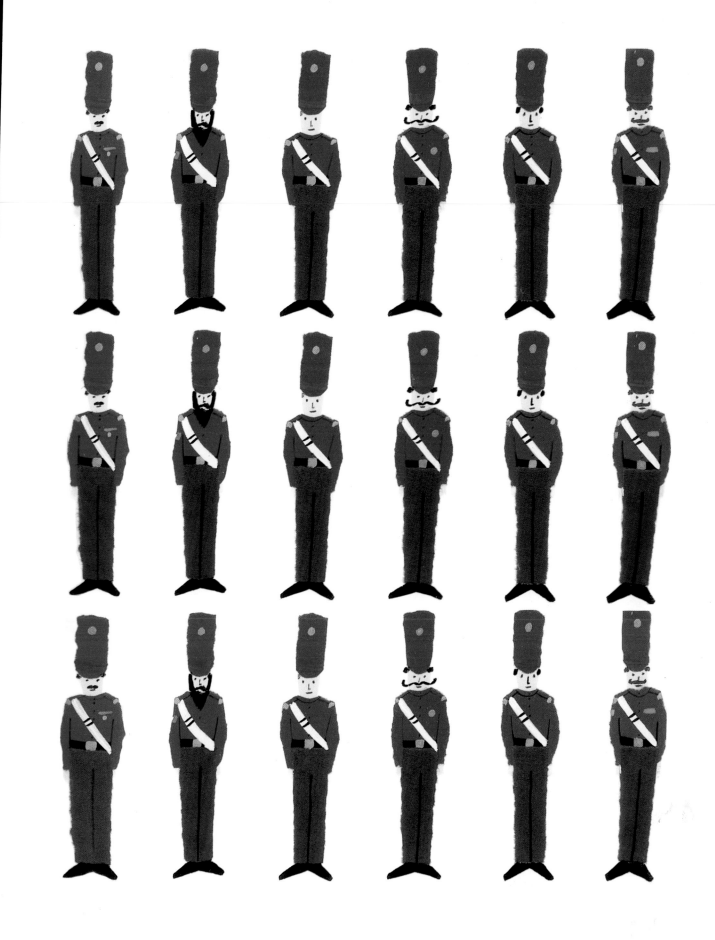

MORE WALKER PAPERBACKS
For You to Enjoy

Also illustrated by Julie Lacome

WALKING THROUGH THE JUNGLE

"An absolute delight… Quite brilliantly, the artist has caught the slightly apprehensive air of the exploring child. As with the best of early years books, there is so much here to look at, to talk about and happily to share." *Children's Books of the Year*

0-7445-3643-X   £4.99

A WAS ONCE AN APPLE PIE
by Edward Lear

A vibrant edition of the classic nonsense alphabet.

"Bright lively illustrations… The smallest toddler will respond to the sounds of this book." *The Daily Telegraph*

0-7445-3146-2   £3.99

THE SHAPE OF THINGS
by Dayle Ann Dodds

"Through simple rhymes this colourful picture book introduces basic shapes – square, circle, triangle, rectangle, oval, diamond – and shows some of the familiar forms they take in the world around us." *Child Education*

0-7445-4368-1   £4.50

I'M A JOLLY FARMER

A lively account of the make-believe games of a young girl and her dog.

"Combines the familiar and the adventurous in just the right way to encourage imagination and pretend play, and has colourful and accessible illustrations. Delightful." *The Sunday Times*

0-7445-4382-7   £4.99

Walker Paperbacks are available from most booksellers, or by post from B.B.C.S., P.O. Box 941, Hull, North Humberside HU1 3YQ

24 hour telephone credit card line 01482 224626

To order, send: Title, author, ISBN number and price for each book ordered, your full name and address, cheque or postal order payable to BBCS for the total amount and allow the following for postage and packing:
UK and BFPO: £1.00 for the first book, and 50p for each additional book to a maximum of £3.50.
Overseas and Eire: £2.00 for the first book, £1.00 for the second and 50p for each additional book.

Prices and availability are subject to change without notice.